Ordinary Men

Extraordinary God

"I do not regard myself as having laid hold of it yet; but one thing I do: forgetting what lies behind and reaching forward to what lies ahead, I press on toward the goal for the prize of the upward call of God in Christ Jesus." Philippians 3:13-14

On the cover are three men on a journey to a mountain top, with a tattered and old trunk left behind. The men represent nine ordinary guys who wrote impactful stories for this book about their past lives before meeting an extraordinary God. They share with transparency their lives before meeting Christ, what it was like to meet Him, and how their lives have been impacted forever on the new journey on which they are still walking.

The trunk represents the old and broken life left behind after accepting God's plan of salvation through His Son, Jesus Christ.

About the compiler and the different writers

Kent McClain, Pastor, School Superintendent, and Teacher, compiled this book from three different groups of men who study the Word of God (Bible) together regularly. They all hold the Scriptures to be without error in the original languages and the Inspired Word of God. They hail from California, Washington, Idaho, and Spain.

The Scriptures cited and referred to come from different versions of the Bible according to the writer's preference.

Ordinary Men   Extraordinary God

US copyright 2025
Published date 2025

ISBN: 978-1-938367-86-1

Published by Destinee Media (www.destineemedia.com)
Cover design by Myrna McClain and Ralph McCall.
Editing done by each writer, and Kent McClain

Table of Contents

	Page
Paul Williams	6
Runner, Teacher, Coach, Part-time Missionary	
Buzz Huget	12
Husband, Father, Businessman, Minister, Grieving Parent	
Ralph McCall	22
Business Manager, Professional Basketball Player, Author and Publisher	
Ric Yorke	34
Husband, Father, Grandfather, Deputy Sheriff, Apprentice of Jesus	
Gilbert Newsom	42
Husband, Father, Businessman, Bible Study Leader	
Tom Wojcik	52
Businessman, Father, and Family Man	

Michael Serapiglia   62

Husband, Father, Grandfather, Civil Designer

Greg Carey   70

Husband, Father, Printing Press Operator,
and IT Support Person

Kent McClain   74

Husband, Father, Minister, Teacher, Superintendent,
Writer/Author

Epilogue   82

Running the Race of Life

Paul Williams
Runner, Teacher, Coach, Part-time Missionary

  I was living the athletic dream in my senior year of high school in Huntington Beach, California. As a track and field athlete, I held several school records in various events. I had the fifth fastest 880 yard-800 meters time nationally as a high school athlete. As a result, college athletic scholarship offers arrived weekly. I was well-liked among my peers and involved in student government. My girlfriend and I were serious about our relationship, and there was even an engagement talk. I was living the dream life, at least I thought I was. However, during all of this, I felt something was missing deep down in my soul. I had achieved all my goals and dreams, yet I still felt empty.
  Things continued as is, though, especially with respect to my running, for I was about to race one of my top competitors. It was May 1968, and the event was the 880-

yard run at the Southern California Track and Field Championships. I was scheduled to race against Greg Jones, who had the fastest time in America this year. Even so, I had never been defeated at this distance and was determined to win this race. The week prior to this race, Greg and I competed against each other in a preliminary race, which I easily won. As the starting gun sounded, we took off at a very fast pace. Eventually, we settled into race pace, and at the 440-yard mark, I found myself three yards behind and began to make my move. The three-yard gap became two yards and then one yard. As we entered the last fifty yards, I moved up even, and the race became a test of will, neither one of us willing to give ground. I could hear the roar of the crowd erupt with excitement as we crossed the finish line together. Unfortunately, I ended up second, but I ran my fastest race ever and ended up with the third-fastest 880-yard time ever run by a high school athlete.

    Yet, my life really did not change much because of this achievement. It was still very much like a Christmas ornament, bright and shiny on the outside but empty and hollow on the inside. Something was still missing, but I had no way of identifying what it was.

    Sad to say, my family was very dysfunctional and extremely chaotic, full of alcohol and drug addiction, promiscuity, and even murder. The daily drama was so constant that I would isolate myself in my bedroom to avoid the never-ending drama. My routine was simple: dinner, homework, pushups and sit-ups, then to bed. Unfortunately for me, I became an invisible family member. In addition, my father didn't even attend one of my high school races or one of my track award banquets.

    Therefore, I ended up being a young man who was always trying to prove his worth in life and constantly needed affirmation. During this time, three questions continually occupied my mind: What is the meaning of true love? Is there a personal God? Does life have any purpose at all? I wasn't very religious because I had appointed track and field as my god, so I didn't expect any answers to come from this venue, or if I did, I was greatly disappointed when it didn't.

Out of the scholarship offers I received, I accepted one from UCLA, one of the best track programs in the country. I had a great year in my first year at UCLA, but for whatever reason, I decided to break up with my high school girlfriend. This decision surprisingly devastated me at first and, of course, broke her heart. I ended up as confused as ever about what true love was all about, and it was my fault.

As I continued to run and compete, I developed an inflated ego, believing that I was a very special person. Over the course of my first year at UCLA, I became more and more self-absorbed and selfish; then, the summer finally arrived, and I returned home to a great job working for Huntington Beach parking lots. Through self-justification, I began stealing money on a regular basis while on the job, as did some of my best friends. One night, I got caught and was fired on the spot. I was devastated, to say the least. It was now difficult to reconcile a good guy image and being known as a thief.

After being fired, I didn't know what to do, so in complete despair, I began walking along the beach, trying to get used to a new image of myself I did not like. On this walk, I fell on my knees and cried out to God, screaming, "God, I need you, please help me." I immediately heard a voice within saying, "Paul, you just got fired. Why would God want to help? You are a lousy thief and unworthy of Him."

As I rose from the sand, I began walking back down the beach in shin-deep water, a broken man emotionally in my spirit and soul. Suddenly, I felt an unexplained presence and heard another voice. This "voice" began to encourage me not to give up that things would get better in the future. As I walked in the water, this "voice" kept encouraging me.

When I returned to UCLA for my sophomore year, I was in tremendous running condition. After being fired from my summer job, I had lots of time to train, and I did just that with great passion and energy. Unfortunately, I also arrived on campus, lonely and empty in my soul as ever. Then I met a girl named Judy, an attractive girl I met near the end of my freshman year. At first, we very much enjoyed each other's company as friends and nothing else. As it happened, we ended up declaring the same major and often had classes together. On occasion, we would walk to and from class together, talking along the way.

Regrettably, I began falling back into being my old self again, dominated by ego and self-absorption, which depressed me all the more. However, Judy would often invite me to a campus Bible study being held weekly at a fraternity house called the "Light and Power House." Each time I was invited, I would politely decline. This presented me with a dilemma because I was beginning to have feelings for Judy. One day, Judy's persistence won out, and I finally agreed to attend one of those meetings with her. My motive for attending was simple; I just wanted to spend more time with her. I knew that this meeting was important to Judy, so what could it hurt to tag along and check it out?

So, there we sat at a Bible study with thirty-five other students, listening to a speaker (Hal Lindsay) talk about being "born again." As I sat and listened, much of what was said began to make sense. Slowly, those questions I had about God, true love, and the meaning and purpose of life were answered one by one. I heard that I had a Heavenly Father who loved me and had a special purpose for my life. That blew me away, for my dad never once told me that he loved me. I heard that God's love is a supreme love that invests in a person's life with no strings attached. Sadly, the only love I knew was to use another person for personal pleasure because of what they could do for me.

While sitting there at this Bible study, I was amazed; the love of a father, for which I was so starved and desperate, was waiting for me to embrace and receive; it was mine for the accepting. I now understood that my personal sin had separated me from God. And no one had to convince me that I was a sinner. All I had to do was, by faith, thank God for sending His Son to die on the cross for my sins and believe in Him as Lord and Savior. Suddenly, the guilt and shame I had been carrying was lifted and forgiven. Even though I still had so many other questions, I asked Jesus into my heart that night.

Of course, Judy was thrilled with my decision, and we continued to date and ended up marrying later. We have been together for 53 years. School teaching and coaching track wound up being my career. In the early years of our marriage, we went behind the Iron Curtain to smuggle Bibles to persecuted Christians in communist countries. We were so nervous at first in doing this, having to trust the Lord every inch of the way. Yet, when we saw the faces of those receiving these Bibles, it was worth it all.

During retirement, Judy and I continued ministering to others, especially to missionaries and persecuted Christians in Colombia and South America. We flew there often, helping in any way we could. The drug cartels in that area of the world had been forcing the indigenous peoples off their lands and kidnapping their young boys and girls, forcing them to work in the cocaine fields and worse. Some of the children who managed to escape were living in a children's center that would care for them physically, emotionally, and spiritually. It is at one of these centers that Judy and I spent most of our time ministering.

BUT THAT'S NOT THE END OF THE STORY THERE IS MORE

Cancer is a very scary thing to encounter, a journey no one wants to experience, but I had to. One day, while working out in the gym, as I usually did, I began struggling, having difficulty breathing and feeling quite weak. Following a few blood tests, I was sent to a urologist and learned that I had prostate cancer. My doctor mentioned that

I would have died within two years if my cancer had not been diagnosed.

For my cure, I underwent 42 radiation treatments that worked but left me exhausted. It felt like running a 26.2-mile marathon every week. What I didn't know at the time was that this cancer was masking a potentially more dangerous heart condition. As I was recovering from my cancer treatments, I seemed to get worse, especially with respect to not having much energy or strength at all. Over the next several months, I struggled even to do the smallest of things, like yardwork. This left me with great feelings of despair and hopelessness. To counter these negative feelings, I often would quote Scripture to myself and pray. One of my favorite Scriptures was Isaiah 41:10, "Do not fear, for I am with you; do not anxiously look about you, for I am your God. I will strengthen you, and surely I will help you, surely I will uphold you with My righteous right hand."

After my cancer was in remission, I sought advice from my primary doctor, who made an appointment for me with a cardiologist. I went through one test after the next, but there seemed to be nothing wrong with my heart. Then, I visited another cardiologist who was determined to get to the bottom of what was wrong. Praise God for her! It would have been easy for this doctor to say come back in two weeks from now, and we will reevaluate your progress. Had she done that, I would most likely have died of a massive heart attack. Instead, two days later, she put me in the hospital for one last test, which would only take about 15 minutes. To her surprise, she found that one of my main heart arteries was 95% blocked. She immediately put in a stint, which saved my life.

Finally, I guess God had my life in His hands from my early days as a young runner to most recently as a retired schoolteacher and part-time missionary. Admitting my sins and receiving Christ as Lord and Savior was key for me and will be for you if you haven't made that decision yourself.

Hope Given; Hope Needed

Buzz Huget
Husband, Father, Businessman, Minister, Grieving Parent

It was Finals Week in the Spring quarter of 1972. I was living in the University District and attending the University of Washington. The next day was my last final. I had studied all I could and knew I just needed to go to bed, sleep, and get after it in the morning. However, going to sleep was usually a problem for me. And this night was no different. As I prepared for bed, worry and fear again crept in and began to well up inside. I was haunted by the same fear, "If I died during my sleep, would I go to heaven"? I didn't know.

I attended church off and on as a child. I even went to our church's Jr. High Spring camp. I knew about Jesus and liked Him. My church had given me a KJV Bible (King James Version) in Sunday School, and I tried reading it many times. I liked the Gospels and could understand them, although they were a little weird. However, when I read beyond them or got into the Old Testament, very little made sense to me.

Growing up, I was the youngest of three boys. My two older brothers played football in high school and went on to play at the UW (University of Washington). I played baseball. I had close friends, but because of my brothers, I was highly recognized on the school campus. After all, I was a "Huget" I surmised. Yet, when I graduated, I took a different path than my brothers and attended WSU (Washington State University).

During this time, our nation was in the middle of the Vietnam War. Every young man turning 18 was very aware of the draft. Up until 1969, if you attended a university, you could get a draft deferment, allowing you to be safe from military service until graduation. Then things changed on December 1, 1969, due to a draft lottery. This eliminated school exemptions, making just about all young men draftable according to a lottery and their corresponding birthdates. I ended up with number 72, which meant I was very high on the list to get drafted. So, I had a decision to make. Do I take my chances of getting drafted with such a high number, or do I choose joining the Washington Air National Guard? I chose the Guard and was soon sent to boot camp in Texas and a tech school in Biloxi, Mississippi.

While in tech school, my brother's wedding was scheduled in Seattle, which I very much wanted to attend. It seemed impossible for me to get out of training to do so. Therefore, I decided to pray that God would make this happen, and if He did, I would serve Him for the rest of my life. The bottom line is my superior officer gave me permission to attend, and off I went to Seattle for the wedding.

On my flight, I had to wear my uniform to get a military discount, and I drank a lot on the way, which was not a very good "thank you" to God for making all of this happen. I arrived in Seattle quite drunk, with a swearing mouth beside. My mother was not impressed. After the wedding, I returned to complete my training and was stationed back in Seattle.

Thereafter, my obligation to the Guard was only one-weekend meeting a month and a two-week summer training obligation. Somehow, though, when I returned to Seattle, I was not quite the partygoer I once was. In fact, my life seemed a little off-kilter, and I did not know why. To get things back to normal, I decided to go to Community College, and while there, I finagled my way into the University of Washington by switching my major to science. Unfortunately, I had to take a chemistry class due to making this change, and I hated it. When my final came, I knew I was in trouble, but because there were 400 in the class, I was able to sneak in a friend who knew chemistry to take it for me. Through his last-minute help, I passed and transferred to a business major for the next semester.

Yet, being back in school didn't really help as I thought it would; I still felt a bit off-kilter. My beliefs about God had not changed, which, as I look back, were not very comforting or accurate. Somewhere along the line, I had come to believe that if I weren't actively trusting Jesus when I died, I'd go to hell, and I didn't want to do that. And so my fear of death continued to grow. My only counter to this was that most nights before I went to sleep, I prayed the only prayer I knew: "Now I lay me down to sleep, I pray the Lord my soul to keep, and if I die before I wake, I pray the Lord my soul to take." This helped me get through the night, but what about the day?

I did have one incident that shook me but didn't change me. In the spring quarter, while crossing the Spokane St Bridge into West Seattle, I started complaining to God, assuming He was listening, about how off-kilter I felt. At the height of my rant, I pounded on the steering wheel. Afterward came a quiet voice, which I know now was from the Lord, "I gave you who you are, but can take all of that away." I was stunned, which elevated my fear of death all the more.

So, back to that night before my final, I once again closed my eyes and repeated my old prayer, "Now I lay me down to sleep..., but before I could finish, I somehow believed in who I was praying to for the first time. I believed Jesus to be real and that He had heard my prayer and accepted it. As I laid my head on my pillow for the night, I knew I had been heard and forgiven. When I awoke the following day, I was amazed that peace had replaced my ever-present fear of death. And with it, came an assurance of Jesus' forever presence.

Later while on campus, I ran into Paul, an old high school friend of mine. I cautiously told him that I thought I was a Christian; I was sure he would think I was crazy. But, not so, for he assured me of my faith. He then told me that earlier that quarter, he had run into Mark, another high school friend of mine, and they both decided to pray for me about Christ and my salvation. I didn't know what exactly that meant, but it sure made me happy.

A few days later, I saw Paul again, and he told me I needed to go back to our old church with him. The church had a new Youth Pastor, Kent, and I should go to his Bible study. It sounded nutty to me. My idea of a Bible Study was a bunch of old ladies sitting around drinking tea out of little dainty teacups and reading that incomprehensible KJV Bible. However, I had been so overwhelmed with experiencing the reality of faith in Christ that I said I'd go. The Bible Study was in the basement of the church, and it felt weird to return there. Plus, it was a study mainly for the high school group. Ultimately, all that didn't matter, for eventually, the group transitioned into being for both high school and college-age students.

During the Bible study, Kent focused on the Book of Romans, using a translation I had never heard of, *The New American Standard Bible*. I was captivated by this translation. It was so readable, capturing my heart with its powerful content and truth. Every week, I could not believe how Romans addressed who I was and what I needed. Over the weeks and months of attending, many lifelong friendships were formed, including one with Lisa, who later became my wife.

After coming to faith in Jesus Christ and studying the Bible for several years, I found I identified with the biblical character, Jacob, whose name means 'heel-grabber,' recorded in Genesis 25. Before coming to Christ, I thought I was clever enough to get what I wanted. In high school, because I was a "Huget", I had unearned status, and with my two older brothers, I could afford to be a smart aleck. My Air Force request for an early leave was sincere, just like my vow to God. If He helped me get home, I'd serve Him, but once that happened, I quickly and stealthily pretended to forget my vow. I was able to rationalize that the vow was, after all, a bit rash, and I figured I probably would have gotten the leave without God's help. And after all, God was probably too busy to remember it. At least deep down, I hoped He had forgotten it. I then spent a year wrestling with my fears of death and hell. But like Jacob, I was a "heal grabber," too smart for my own good. That is, until one night before falling asleep, I gave my life to Christ and received His forgiveness.

As I sit here in my 70s, having been a businessman, pastor, husband, and father to four girls, a boy, and 17 grandchildren, I continue to identify with Jacob, who went through many trials and tribulations throughout his life, even after demonstrating faith. The following account, which I conclude with, is what my wife, Lisa, and I have had to battle through, but not alone, for Christ has never left our sides.

On June 11th, 2022, Lisa and I were slowly getting ready for the day. I had retired 5 weeks earlier from my role as Pastor of Mercy and Mission at our church. Our daughter Abigail lived in our downstairs apartment. That morning, we noticed her parked car, indicating she hadn't gone to work. Lisa called to see how she was, but it went to voicemail. Curious, Lisa went down to see if she was alright or just sleeping in late. A minute later, I heard a blood-curdling scream, and Lisa cried out, "It's Abigail; I think she's dead!"

From that moment on, our lives have been permanently altered. Stunned, it felt like we had dropped into a riptide and earthquake all at once. We couldn't take in or keep up with what was happening. I made the call to 911. Half my brain and mouth were giving details to the operator so he could send the proper help. The other half of my brain was fighting with disbelief and denial over what I was saying. Then, there was Lisa, in a state of shock and emotionally short-circuiting. To this day, she remembers very little of those first 36 hours and has no memory of finding Abigail. I was able to get Lisa back upstairs and on a couch. When the Fire Department arrived, I had to let them in the downstairs sliding door entrance. I pointed them to Abigail's bedroom, where she was, and answered multiple questions which I had no idea what they were. Next, the police arrived. During this time, Lisa made calls to our three daughters. How she did it and what was said remains a fog to her. More police arrived, and they asked permission to search her room and apartment. They need to rule out foul play or drugs. I answered their questions, which only added to the avalanche of information my brain was trying to keep track of and make sense of.

Family members arrived throughout the day, which was comforting. But with each arrival came the intensified reality that 'Abigail is gone.' Because of shock, Lisa would, from time to time, turn to me with wounded eyes and, in bewilderment, ask, "Is Abigail dead?" Each time, she would re-live the painful 'yes.' Later, the Coroner arrived again with more questions. He explained what would happen next, and Rebecca, our 2nd daughter, helped to guide us. He explained to her that he would need to take Abigail's body to determine the cause of death. Finally, he asked if we'd like to see her before she was taken. "No!" was my emphatic answer. Somehow, despite the swirl of the day's events, that answer came to me clearly and with conviction. I didn't want that to be the last picture left in our minds of our daughter. That had to have come from the Lord.

As the day advanced, a new question arose: what about Abigail's son Will? He had recently entered a Men's Drug and Alcohol Recovery Program. He was still in the probationary period, so he didn't have access to his phone. I knew he had to be told in person, and I knew he needed to hear it from me. So, my son-in-law Micah drove us to the facility. We found a quiet spot and told him his mom was dead. There is no preparation or perfect script you can pull out to give you the words. Amid that emotionally dark place, I stumbled forward and trusted God to give me the words I needed. I don't remember the specifics of what I said to Will, but it was again the horrible confirmation of saying out loud, "Will, your mom is dead." We must have wept, but I don't remember. I do remember the three of us standing and holding each other for a long time. I was so grateful that Micah was there to help bear the weight of that moment. Will was able to spend the remainder of the day with the family, and someone took him back to the facility before curfew. Also, at some point in the late afternoon, our son Ricky arrived from San Diego. As the day ended, many friends and extended family members stopped by. The day remains in my mind a swirling mass of faces, snippets of conversations, and emotions disembodied from any category my mind could place them in.

A few days later, we needed to put together an obituary for Abigail. It was one more task that was mentally and emotionally nonsensical. I knew what obituaries were, but how could I connect them to our daughter? It had to be done, and we couldn't leave it to someone else, so we pushed forward. We became stuck, however, by addressing the basic question people would have: how did she die? This meant I needed to call the coroner. We were told it would take several weeks for the official report to be filed but were encouraged to call if we had any questions. I was able to speak with the coroner. He had determined that Abigail died of massive internal organ failure brought on by alcohol withdrawal (my layman's explanation). She must have decided to stop drinking 'cold turkey' without realizing that she would need to go through 'detox.'

Our first reaction was not to mention the cause of death. We didn't want people to think poorly of her. But later, Lisa asked me if we didn't want it to be mentioned because we were ashamed of her. The more we thought about it, the more we concluded we loved her for who she was, all of her. We also concluded that we couldn't control what people thought of her or us. Therefore, we weren't going to pretend she was a saint nor ignore why she died. So, at her memorial service in August, we had Pastor David Lee read the obituary that included the cause of death. That allowed me to give a message about her life that was filled with her joys and sorrows, as well as her loves and failures. Here's one small section of what I shared that day, *"Abigail was loved...but we never called her Saint Abigail. She understood the rough side of life. And she could spit in its eye, speak her mind, and give as good as she got. But because of the tough things she faced, she also understood the secret of love. A love that is self-giving. The self-sacrificing love for others. And she loved her nieces and nephews, her 'babies'. We never called her St. Abigail, but she will forever be their Auntie Abi."*

During the two and a half months between Abigail's death and the memorial service, Lisa and I read *Beyond the Darkness* by Clarissa Moll. Of all the excellent insights she shares regarding grief, the one with the most significant positive impact on us was learning to understand and accept grief as a 'companion.' She helped us see that, over time, grief will change, that it has a mind of its own, and that it will continue to be with us.

In the weeks following the memorial service, I had a growing compulsion to understand grief and lament. I began by reading Michael Card's *A Sacred Sorrow*. He states on page 123, "(We) lament because we cannot understand how a God of *hesed* could possibly allow us to experience pain.

The cause of all laments is an inconsistency between the perceived action of God and the revealed character of God as defined by the word hesed. It is the source of the complaint as well as the solution." He explains that the Hebrew people had a name for this expectation and experience of God's care. It is *hesed*. *Hesed* is most often translated in English as 'lovingkindness.' He then explores lament in the lives of Job, David, and Jeremiah. That began my year-long biblical deep dive into the lament in each of these men. With Job, we read the incredible depth of pain and suffering he expresses to God yet is met with silence. With David, lament is expressed in the great breadth of his life's losses and griefs. He expressed these in his Psalms of Lament. And finally, the Prophet Jeremiah learned the personal cost of lamenting because he learned to lament for unrepentant people. He became the 'weeping Prophet' to stiff-necked rebellious people who were unwilling to repent. I recorded my thoughts and conclusions in my paper, *Lamenting & God's Hesed*.

October 22, 2023, was Lisa and my first time back to church, sixteen months after Abigail's death. As we walked there, I felt my heart nervously pounding in my chest. About a block from the church, we ran into a family. They said, 'Nice to see you guys; what did you do over the summer?' And so began the painful process of us trying to discern, 'Don't they know about Abigail's death, or do they know and are afraid to say anything?' We entered the building and made our way to a pew. Several folks acknowledged and greeted us. During the music portion of the Service, I found myself unable to engage in singing. It was too happy and victorious. Following the Service, there were more greetings of, "How you are doing", "How have you been", "What have you been doing", 'I've missed seeing you", "I've been thinking of you." And several conversations ended just shy of them saying, "Let's get together." In many ways, it felt like people were glad to see us because it made them feel better that we were back and OK. Lisa and I came away convinced that the church needed to understand grief.

This has brought us to a new phase of living with this companion of grief. It has us wanting to help the church evaluate how pastors and worship leaders can lead their congregations in light of loss and lament. Not just to acknowledge it or provide classes, teachings, or outside resources but to incorporate lament into worship. After all, a third of the Psalms, which was Israel's songbook, are Psalms of Lament. And so, in early 2024, I began working on a project, *Lamenting Is Needed in The Church*. What will become of it, and what impact will it have on our local church? Only time will tell. But I am hopeful that in the Lord's redemptive work, He has a plan for some good out of Abigail's death, which will also bring Him glory.

Finally, in all of this, through the birth of my salvation to the passing of my daughter, Christ has never left my side, nor will He ever. He was the hope given to me in 1972 and the hope Lisa and I needed in 2022. That's His promise to me and will be His promise to you.

For Christ Himself said, "I will never leave you nor forsake you." Hebrews 135

Email: buzz.huget@gmail.com

Lost and Found: A Life Transformed

Ralph McCall
Business Manager, Professional Basketball Player, Author and Publisher

I'd like to share my spiritual journey. The simple version goes like this: A young guy was lost, drifting through California. He sought God, and Jesus found him. That changed everything.
But let me expand on that.

I grew up in California, which was the place to be. There was a mystique about it-everyone wanted to be there. The music of the time captured that feeling–*California Dreamin'* by The Mamas and The Papas, and *California Girls* by The Beach Boys. It was the golden land of promise. Young people hitchhiked there from all over the United States to live their dreams, but most often, their expectations were far from met.

At that time, something big was happening in the culture. By the mid-to-late 1960s, California was shifting from Modernism, which believed that humans could define universal truth, to Postmodernism, where truth became relative. "You create your own belief system, your own morality," they said. And "What's right for you is right for you, and what's right for me is right for me." But the Judeo-Christian worldview stood apart–it said that truth wasn't something we invented. It was an absolute, found in a sovereign Someone we could know. And that truth would set you free.

California shaped me. It was a place where truth, and morality were becoming relative, order giving way to fragmentation and chaos. The streets were a battleground of ideologies–hippies, surfers, the Black Panthers, peace activists chanting "Make Love, Not War," civil rights activists, feminists, Eastern mystics, psychedelic seekers, and the Jesus Movement. Each group passionately called for allegiance.

I was caught in the middle of it all. Confused. Searching. Rebellious and getting into trouble.

I was an only child, and we moved a lot. Every year, I was the new kid in school, the one without friends, the one they picked on. That impacts how you see the world. It made me awkward around people, the strange guy, and it turned me into a loner. Church was a part of our lives, but it was rigid and legalistic. God's favor was something you earned by following rules, and those rules kept changing. If you broke the rules and "backslid," you had to get resaved. I tried to be a "good guy for God," but I always failed. Eventually, I gave up. I believed God was real, but He felt far away–unreachable.

As an older teenager and young adult, I drifted. No direction, no purpose–just moving from one thing to the next, never settling. I took whatever work I could find-- construction, lumber mills, odd jobs that never lasted.
But one job stands out.

I worked the night shift at a gas station in one of the roughest parts of Los Angeles. It wasn't the kind of place where people stopped for friendly conversation. It was a place where desperation clung to the air like the stink of gasoline, where trouble didn't just lurk in the shadows-it walked right up to you.

On my first night, my boss, a grizzled man with dead eyes, handed me a .38 revolver. He didn't offer a word of encouragement, no advice on how to handle the customers-just the cold gun in my hand and a simple, chilling statement: "Here. You might need this."

For two years, I worked with that gun tucked into my belt, its weight pressing against my hip like a reminder of how quickly things could go wrong. I saw it all–drifters, hustlers, junkies, men with hollow eyes and shaking hands looking for their next fix. After midnight, the city changed. The everyday folks disappeared, and the streets belonged to the desperate and the dangerous.

Twice, men pulled knives on me. Both times, I talked my way out of it, my heart hammering in my chest long after they left. But the worst came one night around three in the morning.

The office door at the gas station creaked open, and a man stepped inside. He moved with an eerie, jittery energy, his eyes darting around the room like he was trying to spot threats that weren't there. That's when I saw it–the pistol tucked into his belt, its white handle almost glowing under the harsh fluorescent lights.

He was high on something. His pupils were blown wide, sweat beading on his forehead.

I was seated behind the desk in the office, my own gun already in my hands, hidden just beneath the desktop. My pulse pounded in my ears. I could taste the fear in my throat.

I forced my voice to stay steady. "Turn around and walk out, or you'll regret it."

His eyes snapped to my hands, and though he couldn't see my gun, he heard the click as it was cocked. He hesitated.

For a moment, the whole world held its breath.

Would he go for his weapon? Would I have to shoot?

Every muscle in my body was coiled, ready. My finger hovered over the trigger. If he so much as twitched toward his gun, I would have to raise my gun above the desk and fire first.

Then, somehow, sense broke through the fog of whatever drug was controlling him. His shoulders sagged. He exhaled sharply. And without a word, he quickly turned and walked out.

The second he was gone, I let out a shaky breath and set the gun down on the desk, my hands trembling. I felt sick.

I could have killed someone. Or maybe he would have killed me.

I sat there for a long time, staring at the door, wondering how close I had come to either dying or taking a life. The thought haunted me for the rest of the night. Previously I had a couple of near-death experiences, but this one made me wonder what happens after death. Are we reincarnated? Is there nothingness, or is there heaven and hell? And I wondered if someone up there in the sky was looking out for me.

And in the days that followed, a new fear settled deep in my gut–was this my life now? Was I always going to be one bad night away from a bullet?

Back then, trouble seemed to find me wherever I went, but honestly, I can't blame it all on external factors. I enjoyed doing pranks, getting into mischief, and, worse, living outside the rules. In a way, I was like an airplane without a pilot.

One night, after basketball practice at a local junior college, I was waiting for a friend to join me. We were going to go bowling. The street was quiet except for the occasional car humming by in the distance. I was lost in my thoughts when I heard heavy footsteps approaching.

I turned just as a tall guy about my size stepped into my space. He wore a black leather jacket, and his breath reeked of alcohol, and his eyes were wild. I'd never seen him before.

"You think you can steal my girl?" he spat, his voice slurring with anger.

"What?" I frowned, taking a step back. "I don't even know who you…!"

Before I could finish, he grabbed the front of my sweater and yanked hard, the fabric tearing with a sickening rip.

Adrenaline surged through me. My instincts kicked in. I didn't want a fight, but I wasn't going to stand there and let him pummel me, either. In a split second, I twisted his arm while kicking him hard in the you-know-where and then swept his legs out from under him. He hit the pavement hard, groaning.

That should have been the end of it. But then, out of nowhere, two policemen appeared, their batons raised.

"Break it up!" one of them barked.

Before I could explain, the guy on the ground staggered to his feet, eyes blazing. But he wasn't coming for me this time–he turned on the officers, swinging wildly.

That was a mistake.

In seconds, he was slammed back on the ground, his arms twisted behind his back. One of the policemen turned toward me and lifted his baton.

"Wait, I didn't start this," I protested.

The officer wasn't interested. "Save it for the station."

Minutes later, the police van door slammed shut behind me, trapping me in a cage of cold steel. My mind raced as we drove through the dark streets. Was this really happening? Was I about to have a criminal record?

The station smelled like sweat, stale coffee, and regret. A heavy iron door clanked open, and I was shoved inside a small, windowless cell. The moment the door shut behind me, the sound of the lock echoed in my skull.

I was alone.

I sank onto the hard bench, staring at the stained concrete floor. Dread settled in my gut.

Would trouble follow me my entire life? No matter how far I ran, no matter how hard I tried to stay out of it, I always seemed to end up in the middle of chaos.

An hour crawled by each minute stretching into eternity.

Then, finally, the door clanged open. One of the officers stood there, arms crossed. "You're free to go. We saw the whole thing. You were defending yourself."

Relief washed over me as I stepped out. The other guy wasn't so lucky. He had attacked the police. He'd have to go to court.

As I walked away from the station, I felt hollow. The night air, once crisp and clean, now felt thick, suffocating. I should have felt grateful that I wasn't the one facing charges. But all I could think about was the feeling in that jail cell, the solitude, the hopelessness. Was my life to be trapped like that? Is there something more?

How many more close calls would there be?

Would I ever outrun the trouble that seemed determined to find me?

I was in and out of universities, and I was sometimes asked to leave (I'll let you read between the lines). At one legalistic Christian university, the Dean of Students was a stern, authoritarian figure who reveled in the power he wielded over students, seeming to find joy in demeaning them and showing no empathy or genuine concern for their well-being. His sole purpose was to enforce the school's strict moral code, often accusing students of sins and scrutinizing their every action with a cold, piercing gaze. As a lonely, lost guy, all I needed was kind, wise counsel. And genuine love. If the Dean and the school were examples of Christianity, I wanted nothing to do with it.

I hung out with the wrong people. Academics weren't my focus–sports and the beach were. I misused relationships, which I regret. If you'd asked me what I wanted in life, I would have said, "To play volleyball on the beach."

Yes, pure and simple, that was my goal: to hang out at the beach forever. Nothing more.

But something was missing. My life felt empty.

Desperate for answers, I turned to philosophy. I read Schopenhauer, a German thinker known for his pessimism. He basically said, *"Life is meaningless, so expect disappointment"*. That resonated with me at the time.

Then I read that the Book of Ecclesiastes had influenced Schopenhauer. Curious, I picked up a Bible. The final verse of Ecclesiastes struck me: *"Fear God and keep His commandments, for this is the whole duty of man."*

That hit hard. I knew I couldn't keep His commandments-I had already failed. God felt far away. One night, sitting alone on the beach, staring at the vast ocean and the stars, I whispered, "God, if You're real, please show Yourself to me."

And He did.

Not in a bolt of lightning, but through people. Christians started showing up in my life, telling me about God's love. Not the rigid legalism I grew up with, but something different. They spoke of grace.

One of them was a guy named Kent McClain. We met on a basketball court. He was tough and competitive–just like me. During a heated game, I accidentally split open his chin with my elbow. Well, maybe it wasn't accidental. Feeling guilty, I went with him to the hospital. After he got stitched up, he turned to me and said, "You ever thought about Jesus?"

I threw up objections. "Look at all the wars caused by Christianity. Look at all the scandals caused by preachers and priests."

But Kent countered, "God doesn't approve of those things. Jesus was different. Have you considered Him, who He was and what He did?"

That conversation changed everything.

Eventually, I realized I didn't have to perform for God. Jesus had already done everything for me. I understood that Jesus took the rap for all my shortcomings and failures. He died for all my sins, past, present, and future. By accepting this, one becomes a child of God, and God says, *"I will never leave you or forsake you."* I no longer had to gain God's favor by being a good guy for him, and the relationship shifted. It became one of love and trust. The weight of my failures lifted.

I accepted what Jesus did for me and gave my life to Him.

Kent and I became close friends, and we joined the Jesus Movement. We attended a Bible school near UCLA called the Jesus Christ Light and Power House (a name that perfectly fit the era). The teachers there had Baptist backgrounds. There, I learned that the Bible is the Word of God, and my faith in Jesus deepened.

Through that school, I met Linus Morris, who was putting together a Christian basketball team to play across Asia. Little did I know that joining that team would send me on a new trajectory, although I sensed that God was doing something. That trip opened my eyes beyond California. God was leading me to a new land.

Later, I studied at L'Abri, a Christian study center in Switzerland founded by theologian Francis Schaeffer. He taught about worldviews and bringing all areas of life under the Lordship of Christ. There, I met a Swiss nurse named Catherine. She had grown up in a small village in Alsace, France, where her parents started an orphanage after World War II. Her music was Bach and Beethoven, while mine was The Beach Boys and The Beatles. We were opposites but united in faith. We fell in love and got married.

After a basketball tour through Africa, Catherine and I spent our honeymoon in Israel, living for nine months on a kibbutz. I played in the Israeli first division. The people on the kibbutz were kind to us, and the experience of being in

Israel gave me an appreciation for God's plan for the Jewish people.

Returning to Europe, I played professional basketball, earned an MBA, and later a Doctorate from British universities–not bad for someone who once didn't take studies seriously. That led me into the corporate world, working for Hewlett-Packard in Geneva, Switzerland. My territory spanned all of Europe, Africa, and the Middle East. Hundreds of people reported to me, and the job exposed me to diverse cultures and worldviews. Catherine and I also helped start a church in Switzerland, which still thrives today.

I had once dreamed of playing volleyball on the beach forever. But God had a different plan–one I never could have imagined.

Through the years, I've seen God's goodness. Life has challenges. I've messed up, but He remains faithful. God didn't say life would always be easy. He said He would be there with us through everything, and we can trust Him.
Catherine and I now have three daughters and nine grandchildren. We live in a chalet in the Swiss Alps, but we are also part of a new church on the island of Ibiza in Spain–a place much like the California of my youth, full of spiritual seekers searching for fulfillment and truth in all the wrong places.

Other than that, I enjoy writing novels, having written more than twenty-five under a pseudonym. I have also helped some Christian writers get their books into print through a publishing company I created called Destinee Media.

Looking back, here's what I know: Jesus wasn't just a figure in history. He is the way, the truth, and the life. And when you seek Him, everything changes.

That lost, confused kid in California? Jesus found him. And that changed everything.

Before finding Jesus, I searched for identity—something solid, something real. I chased after meaning in the world's ever-changing expectations, trying to define myself by what others thought, by whatever felt right in the moment. But none of it lasted. None of it truly satisfied. Without direction, the only meaning in life was to be a beach bum forever.

Then Jesus stepped in, and I consider it a miracle for where he has taken me.

First, He gave me an identity that isn't fragile or fleeting but one that is anchored in something unshakable—Him. I no longer must prove myself. I no longer have to wander, searching for purpose in things that never deliver. My foundation is firm, built on His truth.

And I don't walk alone. I have a guide–One who leads me through the uncertainties, the struggles, and the moments when I don't know what to do next. When I am stuck, when fear creeps in, when life feels overwhelming, I can call on Him. And He answers.

Proverbs 3:5-6 says, *"Trust in the Lord with all your heart and lean not on your own understanding; in all your ways acknowledge Him, and He will make your paths straight."*

I have seen this promise fulfilled time and again, even in the moments when I felt lost, even when the road ahead seemed impossible. He never fails. And what a wild ride, from leaving California to traveling the world, completing graduate degrees, holding high-level corporate jobs, and ending up in the Swiss Alps and the island of Ibiza. But that's nothing compared to the personal transformation that has taken place. Who would have thought? I attribute all of this to God's grace and His guiding hand.

But here's the thing: God isn't just a problem-solver you call on when things fall apart. He isn't some distant figure sitting in the background, waiting for an emergency call to step in. He is present. Always. Take that in for a moment—the sovereign God of creation, the One who spoke the universe into existence, is with you all the time. And He loves you.

Let me clarify one thing. This is not a health and wealth story. Instead, it's a story about one guy who has been redeemed by God.

What about you? Have you ever asked, "God, if You're real, show Yourself to me?"

Because He will.

The Bible says, *"Seek, and you will find. Knock, and the door will be opened."*

Are you willing to take that step?

Rescued, Redeemed, and Re-assigned

Ric Yorke
Husband, Father, Grandfather, Deputy Sheriff, Apprentice of Jesus

    I was raised by my mom and stepfather, "Pop." My earliest memory of church was going to a Four-Square church where Pop played guitar with others. We did not attend regularly; we also went to a Baptist church. Like so many, during the late 1950s and 1960s, the message I got was God was all about what not to do.

    Just after turning five, we were living in the Palmdale/Lancaster area of Los Angeles County. I went in for a hernia repair and had complications, which resulted in three major operations in just three days. I have a faint memory of waking up on the operating table and seeing a large needle coming out of my chest. I had a lengthy recovery period, but being the youngest of three brothers, I had lots of support, and my older brothers, Mike and Aaron, treated me as a normal kid and did not let me get too spoiled.

Pop was in the aerospace industry, and we moved almost every three years. From California, we moved to Oklahoma, back to California, and then to Spokane, Washington. It was in Spokane that we joined the Morman Church. I was about 8 when I was baptized. Later, I was introduced to the story of Joseph Smith and Brigham Young. It never really made much sense, but I kept it to myself, and fortunately, God was guiding me to His truth even though I was doubting a lot. In the 4th grade, Pop transferred back to California, in the El Cajon area. There, our lives changed a lot.

As I got older, I became more aware that things were not well with Mom and Pop. They were arguing more and more. At 11, I started to have more pain in my leg. After lots of tests, there was something wrong with the main artery in my right leg, and I was scheduled for another surgery. Being this young, I was not fully informed of just how serious it was. I needed a transplant in a section of the femoral artery. If a donor could not be found, the doctor would have to amputate my right leg. Looking back, this is where I realized God cared about me. Turns out the surgeon had been in the Korean War, where arterial transplants were perfected. They found a donor, and a 6" section of my femoral artery was replaced. Although the surgery was successful, I had a hard time; I had a reaction to the anesthesia, and I was in so much pain that I could not sleep.

On the second night, lying in the hospital, I prayed a child's prayer: I cried out to God; I said, "God, please, can I just go to sleep?" Within minutes, I felt a warmth come over me. I looked up and saw someone standing at the end of the right side of my bed. I fell sound asleep, without pain, and slept until the morning. Within a few days, I was up walking and home after about 2 weeks. I never told anyone about my late-night visitor, or my pain being taken away. Was it a Miracle? I believe God sent an angel and healed me. One would think that this would cause me to devote my whole life to God. It did not; this was a source of guilt for many years. As you will see, I was fighting God most of my life. But the miracle lasted; I was able to do almost anything physically, even going through the Law Enforcement Academy at age 34.

Shortly after turning 12, Mom and Pop split. Deep down inside, I knew Mom was not like other Moms. We moved constantly. Both my brothers left home. Mike went into the army, and Aaron went back east to live with his biological father. I was left with Mom. She would open a checking account with a minimum amount and then write checks until they were all gone. We would then move out and onto another city. I was left alone a lot. I lived on and off with my maternal grandmother. Many times, as I was growing up, God provided a family who took me in and schoolteachers who saw something in me that I did not see in myself.

I went to 9 different junior highs and three different high schools. I dropped out of school at 17. I needed to get away from my mother, and Brenda, my first wife, needed to get away from her controlling mother. Within 9 months, Crystal, our oldest, was born. I had no idea what it meant to be a father. I knew that I needed to take care of them. We lived in Lake Isabella, in the mountains of Kern County, where I worked as a roofer and installed fencing and other jobs for my stepfather and father-in-law.

At the time (early 1970s), I knew I wanted something different. So, we moved to Bakersfield, and I started junior college. I started a one-year certificate program in appliance repair. One day on campus, I ran into a friend who told me about the Correctional Justice Program, which was designed to prepare you to become a probation officer. I caught the dream, and with that, I soon discovered I could work, take care of my family, and go to school.

I began my search for religion and faith in college. I studied some of the Eastern religions and philosophies. I became reacquainted or, should I say, studied Jesus. As I read the gospels, Jesus challenged my thinking. I realized that

Jesus was much more than Buddha or any other religious leader. The more I compared, the more I realized Jesus was who he said he was, "the truth and the light." To this day, I cannot remember who confronted me or who asked me the question, "So Ric, yea, there is a lot of evil in the world, a lot of people in far-off places who may never know about Jesus Christ, but what are you going to do with Jesus? Do you believe he is who he said he is? The savior of the world? The only way to God? The way, the truth, and the life?" I thought about this for a couple of weeks, and one morning before class, in the small trailer that I shared with my wife and daughter, I accepted Jesus as my personal savior.

The mistake I made was thinking my faith was unique. I did not find a church; I made up my mind that I could do it all on my own. I was very stubborn my whole life and pretty much wanted to do things my way. I fell for the 70s lie that was going around then and believed that "God was my co-pilot."

In the winter of 1976, Sam (Samantha), our youngest, was born. We lived in a small house in East Bakersfield. I was so blessed; I only had two more years left in college until I was sure I would get hired by the Probation Department. Sam was barely 6 months old when Brenda told me she never really loved me; I was devastated. I thought I was going to school to have a better life and see a great future for us. A week later, I came home, and the house was empty. Now, I had to navigate being a part-time dad.

I'm not sure when it started, but I started to be interested in Playboy and Hustler magazines. Since I was single again, I felt free to do whatever I wanted. I had no idea that lust would be the primary strategy that Satan would use to distract and deceive me from listening to and following God.

If there is a knucklehead club, I would be the founding president…selfish could have been my middle name. I married my second wife, Jeanne, in 1978, who had two boys. For a few years, we were a blended family and seemed happy. For almost 3 years, we attended the Word of Faith Center, where I spiritually grew a lot and was introduced to many biblical resources. However, the pastor and his wife split up. Soon afterward, we got a new pastor with no vote from the congregation. He ended up not being a good fit for our church. I did not take all of this very well, because my faith was in the pastor who left, not in God. As a result, I did not regularly attend church for years afterward. I never really blamed God; I just felt that I could not trust anyone in church again, especially a pastor.

I failed in my first two marriages and was not a very good father or stepfather besides. The reason leading to these failures is that I put my career first and my desires over my family. Yet, I had a very successful career in Law Enforcement.

In the early 90s, I met Nada through work and had a very passionate love affair with her. However, we were entirely outside God's ideal relationship. We dated for almost 3 years. During our time together, we discussed God and Jesus. She was raised in a new-age religion but did not know Jesus as Lord and Savior, which prompted me to explain the Gospel to her. I did the best I could and gave her a Bible. I was not ready to make a commitment, and we broke up soon afterward.

During this time, I was assigned to narcotics investigations. I was natural, and my team made numerous significant cases. I was promoted after a year and stayed in that assignment for an additional three years. In early 1995, I was transferred to patrol. I ended up assigned as a Senior Deputy to a busy substation in the Kern River Valley. In 1998, I was transferred back to headquarters in Bakersfield to the Training Division. Although a challenging assignment with great hours, I found myself completely broken; I was 45 and had done it my way all right; there was emptiness inside, and I knew what it was. I had put God and Jesus Christ on the sideline.

One day, when I was returning to Bakersfield from the Kern Valley, usually a one-hour drive, I prayed the whole way as never before. I even pulled over several times, calling out to God. I confessed many sins and told Him that I had tried it my way, and my way sucked. I then asked Jesus to come back into my life. He answered me in a quiet but powerful way. The word I got from Him was, "completely". I repeated it several times in my spirit. Two hours later, back in Bakersfield, feeling for the first time in many years that I could trust Jesus. I was not sure what "completely" would look like, and I was not sure what was next, but with my newfound faith, I knew that God would show me how to follow him with my whole heart. He did and has ever since.

I once again started reading the Bible and going to church. Two or three weeks later, I met Nada at a mutual friend's house. She had changed. She told me how she had accepted Jesus as her personal savior and was attending a local Bible church. We started seeing each other again, and we were engaged just a few months later. She introduced me to Fruitvale Community Church, which later became Riverlakes Community Church. Less than a year later, we were married; that was 25 years ago.

At Riverlakes, for the first time in my life, I began to be discipled. I started attending men's Bible study. I learned how I was supposed to grow, to spiritually mature into the man that God designed me to be. I took classes and studied. I grew a lot during those years. I was part of a small men's group where I was introduced to the "Pure Desire" ministry, which addresses porn use and sexual addiction. That ministry, along with others, has made a big difference in dealing with lust. After all these years, I feel like I have wasted so much time being sidetracked and deceived. I confessed so many times but did not repent. Through both failures and successes, times when I did not give in to temptations, I grew. Slowly, the Holy Spirit taught me to stand firm and to run away from some temptations. Only in the past few years have I come to understand the power in I

Corinthians 10:13, "God will not allow me to be tempted beyond what I can handle, and He, my God, will provide a way out, but I need to ask and wait for His way out, not mine…"

During my time at the Training Division, I was sent to the yearlong school called the "Master Instructor Development Program." I learned not only to teach and instruct better but to teach others how to teach. God is so incredible… little did I know I would use what I learned and practiced in serving the church. At Riverlakes, I first helped one of my mentors, Kent, with simple things like PowerPoint, and he posed questions. One of which has been a lifelong pursuit; "So Ric, if Jesus was successful in making disciples out of ordinary men, should we… you *Ric* do what Jesus did?" I use the word funny for God occasionally because he must have a sense of humor to use me. I sit here almost 25 years later, reading Dallas Willard's book, "*The Divine Conspiracy*," where towards the end of the book, he answers the question, "How to Make Disciples?" Simply put, start with the Gospels. and get what Jesus did and said in your heart.

I was later asked to help develop a curriculum for a discipleship process. Again, God was stretching me and using the years of training for His church. I also served a short stent on staff. One of my true blessings was when I was asked to provide a class on discipleship at our local Rescue Mission's one-year program. After some success, I got two of my brothers, who had been in my small men's group, Gil Newsom and Matt Fountain, to help. The men in the program called us the "3 Amigos". What an honor! I could go on and on about all the blessings we got, but the one I learned the most was from men in the program who we saw week after week and challenged to grow in our Lord. These same men are what most of society counts as lost or worthless. I needed to learn that as an old cop. There are no wasted people in God's economy.

I am now retired, but only from my career in Law Enforcement. Now, I serve the men and the church here in Sequim, Washington. By no means is my life perfect. I am all too familiar with the pain of growing old, the struggle against the flesh, not to mention being surrounded by family and neighbors who are far from and/or are even hostile towards the Gospel. Then there are the losses in this life and the grief that goes with it. Now in my 70s, my parents are gone, many of my partners who I served with, my brothers in arms are gone. The hardest was when my oldest, Crystal, passed away in 2022 from an accidental overdose of prescribed medication. That was so hard, and I miss her a lot. But knowing without a doubt that she is in heaven makes grief so much easier to bear. I simply do not understand how anyone can navigate losing a child or a loved one without God in their lives.

Yet, there is so much to be grateful for, and the feeling, joy, and assurance I now have in Jesus is the best thing this side of heaven. I am learning to love God more and more and understand at a deep, deep level the grace and mercy that God has given me my entire life and how even when I don't want to, God shows me through His word, His spirit, my wife, and my fellow believers, the men I call my Barnabas' that it is Jesus that grows and matures me for His purpose. And that I have a lot more to learn… my apprenticeship continues.

Still in His Grip, Ric

We Are Losing Him!

Gilbert Newsom
Husband, Father, Businessman, Bible Study Leader

I came to know the Lord when I was 37. I don't recall the exact date, but I remember the circumstances. I was on the way to Tehachapi, California, from my home in Bakersfield, about an hour's drive away. During my commute, I was in the habit of searching for a radio station. I usually had the radio tuned to a country and western station from Bakersfield, but as I traveled up the mountain to Tehachapi, I would lose reception. As I was searching for country music, sometimes, I would encounter Christian music or Christian preaching. With little hesitation, I would immediately change the channel because I was uninterested in the music and the message. However, while channel surfing on this day, I kept coming across this station airing an old guy named Vernon McGee, with what seemed to me a familiar way of speaking. I thought of it as an Oklahoma accent. I guess he sounded somewhat like my grandparents. He spoke in a down-to-earth manner, and for whatever reason, his way of speaking appealed to me.

I hated the drive to Tehachapi and the conditions I was working in when I got there. I was not getting along with my business partners, and I was miserable. I grew up in

California and lived here most of my life, except while my dad was in the army. My family was of great importance to me growing up. We had a large family on both my mother's and father's sides. I had over twenty cousins close to my age. My dad always stressed that family was what you could count on and no one else. Both my paternal and maternal grandparents were farm workers who had managed through hard work and sacrifice to become farm owners. The family philosophy was that you either worked hard or were lazy and good for nothing. Along with this belief in hard work was the unspoken message that if you worked hard and provided for your family, as a man, you could pretty much do as you wanted as long as you didn't do drugs or end up in jail.

    I am the oldest of three siblings. My brothers were born two and four years after me. My dad was the catalyst for our family. He was larger than life. He joined the army during the Vietnam War when he was twenty-nine years old, married with three kids! Dad was very loving and had a way of making us feel safe and secure in the world. He was always initiating fun things to do, such as hunting, fishing, and parties. He would bring younger men and women of all ethnic backgrounds over from his platoon and throw big parties. Dad taught us that everyone was equal; what mattered was how you acted, not your race or social status. My mom was also very loving and cared for us as only a good mother does. I believe she didn't always agree with some of the things my dad taught us, but he was so energetic that she found it hard to go against him.

    Some of the things that mom probably wasn't on board with were allowing us to drink at a young age or be promiscuous. Another family trait that was promoted even by my mom was defending yourself physically. I think it was a lot more common than it is now, but my family took it to an extreme level. For some reason, I really took to violently responding to any threat, physical or otherwise. I guess it was a way to seek approval from my family and others.

As fun as my dad was, he was also strict in a lot of ways and probably somewhat overbearing. As I think back on my upbringing, it was a strange combination. One example that I recall was my dad telling me, "You are too smart to bring home C's from school; anything less than a B will result in punishment." I believed him, so I did well in school. I guess this combination of permissiveness in some areas coupled with strictness in others formed a buried rebellious nature within me.

After I graduated from high school, I left Arizona, where my dad was stationed, and moved back to a small town in California to work on my grandparents' farm. I had been told that college was a waste of time unless you knew what you wanted to be in life, so I didn't consider that a valid option.

Life on the farm consisted of long days in the summer sun irrigating, weeding, driving tractors, and whatever else was required of a farm hand. I enjoyed the work, living with my grandparents and working right alongside my grandfather. Working long hours and being somewhat isolated, I didn't have time to go out much after work, but it was during that time that I met my wife, Julie. She was attending her last year of high school when we started dating.

Soon after, my dad got out of the army and went to work with his brother, my uncle Joe. A large aerospace firm in the Los Angeles (LA) area wanted to open a subsidiary to do the centerless grinding operations on the fasteners they manufactured. They bought my uncle's small shop in LA so he could move to Porterville, another small town. My uncle contacted my dad, who was finishing up his term in the army, and asked him to help. He also contacted me and one of my cousins and offered us jobs.

So, we all moved to open the business. It started out with only four of us, but with the backing of the large company in LA, it grew quickly and ended up with about forty employees. It was a crazy time. All the guys we hired were young and wild. Shortly after I began working, Julie graduated high school and moved to Porterville with me. Not long after, we were married, with our first child on the way. I was nineteen, and Julie was eighteen.

We worked ten-hour shifts. As the business grew, we needed a night shift, so I was selected as a foreman for nights. I barely knew what I was doing and was trying to teach other young men how to operate the machinery. It was an exciting time. We would work our shifts and then leave work and often party for hours

During this time, Julie, my cousin Steve, his wife, and I took a trip to LA. We stayed at my aunt's house and visited another cousin who was also our age. That night, leaving the wives at home, we went out to Redondo Beach; Steve and I got into a bar somehow, even though we were both underage. We both got very intoxicated. Out on the pier, I ended up in a fight with some guy. I don't even remember why. During the fight, he stabbed me in the lower back, piercing my right kidney. He began running, and I chased him until I fell down from blood loss. An ambulance picked me up and rushed me to a nearby hospital. As the doctor was working on me in the emergency room, I heard someone say, "We are losing him!" I ended up losing my right kidney, but the doctors saved my life.

I think everyone expected a change in me after coming so close to losing my life. But I didn't change, and if anything, I got worse. After recovering, I returned to work and started running the day shift. I would work all day, and then, many nights, I would party until the bars closed. Eventually, I grew tired of this routine and tried to change it.

The more I tried, the more inconsistent I became. I would slow down on the partying, work out, and get in shape. I even ran in the LA Marathon twice but would always revert to the party life. Fortunately, Julie was the one constant in my life. She didn't drink, do drugs, or party at all. Even when I tried to influence her to do the things I was doing, she held firm. Praise God for Julie.

The aerospace business is historically cyclic to say the least. I like to call it the feast or famine business. It would get incredibly busy, which would require us to hire more people, buy machines, and lease big, expensive buildings. Then, suddenly, the bottom would fall out. We would then have to lay off everyone, sell used machines at a loss, default on the leases, and almost go bankrupt.

My dad and I had always wanted to open our own business, so we moved to Bakersfield in 1991 and opened a shop. We couldn't have chosen a worse time. Soon after we had everything up and running, the industry took a cyclic downturn. We ended up losing the business. Soon afterward, to make ends meet, I entered a partnership with a small fastener company in Tehachapi, not far from Bakersfield.

After a significant amount of time on this particular job, the partnership ended up being a disaster for me. The other end of the partnership was owned and operated by a man and his wife. Now, I usually get along well with people, but I could not get along with this couple. I was miserable and hated my life the way it was. Due to the circumstances, I couldn't turn to my family, for they were all struggling financially also due to the downturn in the aerospace industry.

While driving to work one morning. I tuned into a familiar preacher's voice on the radio; it was Dr. Vernon Mcgee. I listened to him this time around, and when he started talking about Jesus and His redeeming work on the cross, I knew I needed Jesus. So, I asked Him into my life, even though I did not fully understand all that it meant. As I look back now, I believe Jesus did come into my life and saved me right then. Afterward, I experienced a peace I had never experienced before, a peace I still have today.

My life didn't suddenly change in all areas. However, it did begin to change in certain areas. For instance, I began to read the Bible and believe what God tells us in it. I found a Bible-preaching church and a brotherhood of believers to worship and fellowship with. One of the verses that resonates with me due to the changes that went on and are still going on today is Philippians 1:6: "*And I am sure of this, that he who began a good work in you will bring it to completion at the day of Jesus Christ.*"

I still have the sinful man inside wanting to wreak havoc in my life, but now I have the Holy Spirit who always offers and empowers me with the opportunity to choose the life I was meant to live according to God's will.

It was during this difficult time that I became a believer, but I needed the Lord's help more than ever before with this job. I didn't know for sure what the Lord might do in response to my need, but at least I knew for the first time that my sins were forgiven, and I was assured of a place in heaven. In addition to my praying for help, I began to search God's Word, the Bible, for answers and direction.

To my surprise, life did not suddenly become more manageable. If anything, it got worse. I felt like I had lost some of the old tools and methods I had previously used in dealing with people. For example, I couldn't just hate them and work to their disadvantage as I would have before with others. Instead, Christ put within me a new desire to love and even pray for my partners during confrontations. This kind of thinking was new to me and took time to take complete hold. Prior to accepting Christ as Savior, my philosophy was that I and my family would be first and everyone else a distant second. God was not really in the picture.

Nevertheless, in the partnership I had with this man and his wife, they owned and controlled access to the manufacturing building that I was able to move into with my equipment. But I think they were a little wary of me because they wouldn't give me a key to the building right away until I had earned their trust. That should have served as a clue as to the future of our business relationship, for I had never been viewed so suspiciously. It seemed that they were always watching me. Long story short, things went from bad to worse. They finally told me to pack up my stuff and get out. We dissolved the limited partnership.

In my leaving, although painful, they at least did not prevent me from removing my machinery and paid me for some work I had done at the end. I should have seen it coming, but it still shocked me. I was suddenly without a means of income with all the usual expenses, a family to clothe and feed, a mortgage, etc. I remember that night I could not eat or sleep.

Yet, as I awoke each morning, I kept remembering that while going back and forth to work each day to this building I had been kicked out of, I would pass an industrial complex about ten minutes from my house. During those drives, I would pray to God daily, saying, "Lord, I sure would like to have my business there." As I look back now, I see that He was listening to me all the while.

After I wandered around in a daze for a few more days, my wife said, "Well, what are you going to do"? I had been praying to God, "What do I do, Lord?" I never heard a voice from heaven, but I again remembered my prayer about having a business in that industrial building ten minutes from my house. As I continued to think things through, I realized that many reasons and obstacles kept me from going into business again, but I still had that desire. I knew that if I were to follow that desire, I would need help from God. Therefore, I kept reading His Word and praying to Him daily.

He convinced me to take it one step at a time, often not knowing what the next step would be. I believe this is faith or at least walking by faith. I soon leased a small unit within that industrial complex, moved some equipment in, and began again. This time, to the best of my ability, I would do it God's way.

I convinced my dad to come back into business with me even though he had told me many times that he was done with the aerospace business. Meanwhile, I had developed some customers who needed our services, so we began again.

When I became a believer in Christ, my dad was one of the most surprised. He commented that although he had lost his best party buddy, he was happy and proud that I had accepted Christ. Because we worked and spent so much time together, we often began to talk about the Lord. He even began to listen to a pastor I loved on the radio, J. Vernon McGee. Afterward, we would talk about McGee's daily lessons. Dad eventually put his faith in Jesus. Around this same time, my uncle Joe, another previous party partner of mine, turned to the Lord. Eventually, my son and daughter, through their own life crises, also came to believe in Jesus Christ. My wife had been a believer from an early age and had a sound foundation in the Lord.

As for my business, over the years, we stayed in that small unit and slowly began to rebuild. Eventually, we filled the entire unit with machines and maxed out the power available in the unit and an adjoining unit that did not need the power. We ended up with twelve employees running two ten-hour shifts five days a week and a lot of eight-hour Saturdays. We were in that unit for twenty-five years when COVID-19 happened.

The reduced air travel caused the commercial airline business to plummet. The demand for aerospace fasteners also dropped as Boeing and Airbus canceled or deferred aircraft orders. Our business dropped to almost nothing.

So, I began that old familiar process. I had to start laying off our employees. Some had been with us for years. I held on to our essential people as long as I could. I kept our two foremen, my brother, and a few others, but the money just wasn't coming in like it was going out. Fortunately, God blessed us with the wisdom and the ability to stay out of debt this time so we wouldn't go bankrupt like before. This time, I slowly ran out of funds to keep going. I would get a stray job here and there, but nothing to count on. I continued to pray and read my Bible daily. I would ask God, "What do you want me to do? Should I close the shop? Should I continue?"

Finally, I had to choose because of finances and emotional stability. I closed the shop. As I look back at the stressful times in my life, I see God's hand in many ways. It seems to me that I have a hard time letting go of situations in my life, even if they aren't going well for me. Or maybe I think everything is alright, like in the case of our business. I wonder if maybe God stirs the nest and pushes me out when I need it the most. But He never lets me fall all the way to the ground as the following scripture verses promise.

> *"He found him in a desert land and in the howling waste of the wilderness; he encircled him, he cared for him, he kept him as the apple of his eye. Like an eagle that stirs up its nest, that flutters over its young, spreading out its wings, catching them, bearing them on its pinions, the Lord alone guided him, no foreign god was with him." Deuteronomy 32: 10-12*

There are many struggles and snares along the way in life. And through them all, I still was, and still am, a sinner fighting my flesh to do the right thing in many areas of my life. I found Riverlakes Community Church (RCC) three minutes from my house and a band of brothers to fight the fight with. I have also been blessed with Godly men to teach me, like the leader of men's Bible study at RCC, Pastor Kent McClain. I have also served and learned brotherly love from men such as Ric York, Matt Fontaine, Mike Seraphiglia, Dan Barnette, and so many others.

Presently, I am watching for what God will do next with my life. I am retired from the struggles of business, but the battle with the world, the flesh, and the enemy of our soul, Satan, goes on. Yet, I will continue to trust and believe that Christ will see me through whatever is ahead.

It Wasn't Fate; It Was God

Tom Wojcik
Businessman, Father, and Family Man

    In the following words, I hope to explain how God came into my life. It was not a single event but a life full of events and feelings that happened to me over the years. I knew about religion from a few encounters, but no attempt to educate me about God in my childhood years ever happened. In my writing, I hope to show you how God affected my life without me knowing it, and I hope you will look back on your life to see God's effect on it. It wasn't all good luck, bad luck, or fate; it was God.

    I was not raised in a religious home, but my mother and father both attended church as children and their parents were good people. My father was Catholic, and my mother was Baptist, so they could not agree on a church to attend. When I was about six, my grandfather gave each of us a small New Testament Bible with very small print. Later, I tried to read it, but I could not understand it; I still have the

Bible because I knew it was important. When I was nine, we moved to Idaho to a 120-acre homestead, where most of our neighbors were Mormons. This led to my father inviting the missionaries to our home to learn about the LDS teaching. After three sessions, he told them that he had learned enough so not to come back. Once, my father took us to Mass at the catholic church. It was still in Latin, so I did not understand anything. My mother was against us attending, so we never went back.

I always thought that some events in my life were fate, but now I know that those points in my life were God's plan and guidance. God provided the outline of my life, and I, through my free will, filled in the details. When I look back at all the things that happened or decisions that I made in my life, I can see that there was a plan to get me to where I am now.

For instance, I was born in a small town in the state of Washington. When I was only two or three years old, my father told me that he had a car with suicide doors, doors that open to the back of the car, not the front. One day, I was in the back seat as he was driving. I somehow opened the door, and it swung open, caught in the wind with me hanging on to it. He had to reach back and grab me before I fell off into the road. He always said it was a miracle that I did not fall; I think it was God's sovereignty. While I was young, I started going in the wrong direction; I remember going into neighbor's unlocked houses and taking candy, money, and cigarettes. I also set a fire in a field and bullied other kids. When I was eight, God stepped in again, and my father won a farm in Idaho that the government was giving out in drawings to veterans. You can't be a juvenile delinquent when you live on a farm.

My father had promised my mother that we would only stay the two years that were required to stay on the farm, so the farm was his. We moved to Paul, Idaho, a little town eight miles south of where the farm was to be, in the middle of winter, just before Christmas.

Our first temporary home there was not insulated and had an oil stove in the living room/kitchen area for the whole building; in the wintertime, it glowed cherry red. I can still remember lying in bed looking at the metal roof with frost on it, my brother and I in the same bed with lots of covers on us to stay warm.

Because we lived so far from town and school, we rode the bus to and from school. One day, the bus driver stopped at the crossing and looked both ways but could not see to the right because of a potato plant building but proceeded to drive across anyway. I felt an uncontrollable feeling that a train was coming, so I yelled for the driver to stop, and he did, just as the train went by. It would have crushed the bus. I now know that this was God keeping me alive.

My father had great potato crops those first two years, so he convinced my mother to stay. Money was borrowed from FHA, and a new farmhouse was built. The old house turned into the barn and shop that it had been built for.

The next year, during the summer, my mother would drive to town to go shopping and drop all of us kids off at a community swimming pool. On one of these trips going home, as she approached a yield right-of-way intersection of graveled roads, she looked both ways but could not see to her right because of a tall wheat field. She still drove into the intersection. A young man was driving his car down the gravel road at about 60 miles per hour. If he had t-boned our car, we would all have been dead. Instead, we hit him in the side;

I can still clearly recall this incident to this day. We saw the car we hit, and parts of the car started flying, and disappeared in a cloud of dust. When we located the car, it was a total wreck; it had flipped end over end, and there was no driver in it. We found the driver in a ditch beside the road, with a trickle of water in it and the driver's head covered with blood, unconscious, flopping like a chicken with its head chopped off. He had been thrown through the windshield and hit his head in the rear-view mirror. We held him down for a minute, and he stopped moving.

My mom had me run back to the car to have my younger brother run to the farmhouse about a quarter of a mile down the road to call an ambulance. I went back to help her; it seemed forever until the ambulance got there. The young man turned out to be ok, the ditch he landed in had saved his life. Reflecting, it was a miracle we all survived.

I was not a great student in school, but in the 6th grade, my math teacher, Mr. Daley, took me under his wing and helped me learn to study and pay attention in class. In my freshman year in high school, Mr. Simcoe helped me be consistent with my homework and test scores. I think God led my teachers and others to help me become a better person.

In 1964, my father had to sell the farm, and we moved to Twin Falls, Idaho. I was beginning my senior year of high school. We were living in a rented home, and in the neighborhood, I met my future wife, Valery. Meanwhile, a new Junior college, College of Southern Idaho, was starting in Twin Falls, which I decided to go to because it was a lot less expensive, and I could live with my parents. In one of my classes, a friend, Gary, sat by me and happened to mention that he was applying for a summer job at the phone company and that I should do the same. I did and ended up with a permanent part-time job that led to my life-long employment at Mountain Bell, AT&T, and Lucent Technologies. When I look back, I now know this was all part of God's plan for my life.

I got married to my wife, Valery, when I was 20 years old. She was just 17 and Mormon, and as I learned later, we were both too young to know what we were doing. I joined the Idaho National Guard in 1968 to avoid being drafted to Vietnam. I was at Fort Knox, Kentucky, when my first son Shaun was born. We had two sons but, sad to say, divorced within 7 years. I then met my next wife, Vikki, and were married within a year. We had our daughter, Erin, within the next 2 years.

I was now on my third job with Mountain Bell and working hard to get a new job selling data products in Boise. While I was at training, Vikki was overseeing the building of our new house in Boise, arranging our move, and taking care of Erin.

In 1985, after the divestiture of the Baby Bells, I now worked for AT&T. While training for this new company, and on a return flight from Denver, the pilot lost the yaw control of the airplane soon after takeoff. The plane started losing altitude, the cabin filling with smoke, and the wings were dropping up and down. Somehow, the pilot turned the plane around and got us back to the airport with the plane still doing all these crazy things.

Inside the plane, it was almost silent; all I could hear were people praying and telling the person beside them they loved them. I was sitting beside one of the secretaries from our office; we held hands. The flight attendants had us lower our heads in the crash position. Somehow, the pilot levelled off the plane just as we touched down. In the midst of this, there were fire engines and ambulances everywhere as we landed. I firmly believe that God guided the pilot that day to save all our lives.

AT&T went through significant downsizing, and I survived it, getting a better job that led to an even better job as other people transferred and left the company. In the mid-90s, AT&T divested the telephone equipment side of the business creating Lucent Technologies which I became a part of.

By 1999 I was ready to retire, I was 53, stressed out from working six days a week and thought I could get along with my higher-than-average retirement and savings. I was wrong, but luckily Lucent contracted me back to complete some of my major sales implementations for the first year of my retirement. Then by luck, I joined with two retired technicians from Lucent, and we became Associated Technologies LLC.

Through all this time, Vikki was with me, through all the jobs, training, traveling, and not enough time at home. We had good and bad times. I was gone too much, we had problems with our daughter, our parents all passed away, money problems arose, building and selling houses took our energy, and other problems came that long-time married couples have, but we stayed together.

In 2010, Vikki was diagnosed with dementia; she was putting ice-cream in the cupboard, metal pans in the microwave, and gradually losing her ability to speak. I could not travel anymore so for another two years I worked at home doing programming and bids for our company.

People with dementia go through many stages, with Vikki it started slow and then accelerated. For a while it was putting things in the wrong place and not remembering words. She tried doing all kinds of puzzles and mind games to slow the advance of the disease. Then she reversed day and night and wanted to stay awake all night and sleep all day. Then the words that she spoke were all in the wrong order and made-up words. I had to learn a new vocabulary almost every week.

During the wandering period, I had to change the lock on the front door so a key had to be used to open it and Vikki could not get out. When I worked outside, I took her out with me but after a while, I had to tie her to a chair so she would not wander off. She could not feed herself, so I fed her. I did all the housework and stayed home except when my daughter would stay with her. My doctor told me about a care service that would watch Vikki for a day per week so I could go to the store and get away for a little while.

Then in late March 2015 hospice came. In April Vikki passed away, we had been married 41 years. When I was young, I never thought about dying or my loved ones passing away. Then I lost my grandparents, a few friends along the way, and then my parents. I missed them but my life remained mostly the same through these losses. When Vikki died, there was a huge hole in my life and heart. I thought I had prepared myself for this to happen, but there is really nothing I could have done to prepare for this loss and change in my life.

    I was in a daze, not really knowing what to do or where to go. It is the best advice in the world to not make any kind of decision for at least a couple of months when your loved one dies. Your friends and family are there to start with, but they have their own lives to live, and they fade away, so you are left to be on your own.

    I was lucky to have a true friend, Thom Nichols, who stuck with me. Before Vikki died, he would take me to lunch every Thursday when my helper came to watch Vikki while I was gone. After she died, he still took me to lunch and other activities; he stayed with me during my real hard times. I also had my dog, Henry; I took him for two walks every day; this got me out of the house, I got some exercise, and I talked to people on the greenbelt where we walked.

    I started wondering, where did Vikki and my parents go when they died, to Heaven or to nothing?

    Unexpectedly, Jehovah Witness's started showing up at my door, and I invited them in for about three months. Once a week, they came to my home to talk about their church's beliefs. What they were teaching me just did not seem right. Then one day, while walking again on the greenbelt, I started talking to a neighbor named Kent. I knew he had been a minister. So, I asked him, where did Vikki go when she died? He asked me a few questions about her life and then told me her spirit had probably gone to Heaven. The Jehovah's Witness had said she was dead until Jesus came back to this earth, so I liked Kent's evaluation much better.

    He and I talked about what I had been learning, and he offered to start teaching me about the Bible, starting with the book of John. I was ready for this; it was just what I needed at this time in my life. I told the Jehovah Witness to not come back.

I trusted Kent and what he said, I think that is a necessary requirement of the person who is introducing you to the details of the Christian religion. He worked with just me for about six months, we almost got through the book of John, but also discussed God, Jesus, and the Holy Spirit. I was feeling more and more comfortable with Jesus in my life. Then Kent asked me if I wanted to join a group of men who met once a week to do other Bible study, and I decided that I would, for I had reached a time when I felt I could share my beliefs and thoughts with others. So, I joined in, which ended up being a great experience.

I prayed every night on my knees, beside the bed. I prayed for Vikki, my family and for God to help me find a new life. It took about a year, but I was putting my grief behind me and enjoying my life again. I met new people and enjoyed more time with my old friends.

In the summer of 2016, my sister-in-law, Pam, came to visit me and needed a ride to meet the person who had driven her to Boise from Twin Falls. I drove her to the Boise Mall, where she was to meet her friend for lunch, and I decided to go with her. This is the first time I met Margaret Sinclair. She had been Pam's friend since they went to junior high together and was also the sister of one of my best friends in high school, Mike.

When I met Margaret, she had been a widow for almost 10 years. We communicated very well at that lunch. In October, we went to dinner and walked on the greenbelt, and then we started calling back and forth. In November, she came with Pam to my 70th birthday party. We started a long-distance friendship that turned into a loving and supportive relationship.

Margaret was the person I needed in my life and I was the one she needed in hers. God had put us together to answer both of our prayers. Now we are together and traveling the world.

After I sold my house in Boise and moved to Twin Falls to be with Margaret, I could no longer continue my

Bible class, but during Covid, Kent started doing the classes via Zoom, so I could now join back in. This continued until I moved back to Boise and could attend the classes in person again. I had asked Him if he would baptize me, and on July 24, 2022, I was baptized by Kent. I had given this step in my life much thought; through the Bible classes, I learned that God had a plan for my life, and I realized that all the things that had happened to me that I thought were fate and luck were really God guiding me through His plan. When I was baptized at the age of 76, through Kent's guidance, I already believed in God, Jesus Christ, and the Holy Spirit, and I hope to continue my education.

God Works in our Lives but Is Not Always Seen

Michael Serapiglia
Husband, Father, Grand Father, Civil Designer

I was born on September 1963 into a Catholic family in Lancaster, Pennsylvania, and have an older sister. My parents divorced when I was about two, and I had no contact with nor memory of my biological father. Apparently, when you divorce an Italian, you are dead to that side of your family. My sister and I would stay with our maternal grandparents in a suburb of Pittsburg, Pennsylvania, for extended school breaks when my mother was busy with her schooling.

We moved to State College, Pennsylvania, for our mother's continued education at Penn State. This is where my mother met our new father while they were working on their degrees. Later, when I was eight years old, we moved to Arizona.

To be honest, I didn't warm up to having a new father for many years, but I did have a close relationship with my grandparents and a great-aunt who brought us to a Catholic Church. During those years, I remember getting into trouble a lot and finding other misguided boys who seemed good at finding trouble like me. It was like having a secret life that my family knew nothing about until the police brought me home or I ended up in a hospital somewhere.

Most of my life was spent resisting God and His Word. As a young child, God frightened me more than my grandfather! He is my oldest memory and an example of a hard worker. I'm sure he had a compassionate, loving, and tender side, but I do not remember seeing these kinds of emotions in him. I only remember that he was bossy and demanded his way, which I didn't care for. I may have even adapted this as my view of God as a child.

In Arizona, due to my exhaustive energy, I was enlisted in peewee football. I was also busy with a paper route 7 days a week, which helped me learn discipline and responsibility. I did well in elementary school and had several good friends. My parents were doing well financially and wanted to move into a newer home as I was entering high school. Unfortunately for me, I had to leave friends again as we moved across town. I found some new friends at school but didn't fit in with most of the new neighborhood kids, who were more upper-class. I felt out of place in this new high school, not having my childhood friendships and relationships.

During the summer of my sophomore year, the course of my life was changed by a near-death accident. Fortunately, I was young and in relatively good shape, or my physical injuries could easily have been far worse. I was invited to go tubing down the Salt River with a group I didn't know well. I do not recall the day much, but there was drinking and, most likely, drugs involved. It was one of the worst single-car accidents in the area that year. You might be thinking that this is where God finally touched my life, and I submitted to His guidance, but no, I was still running from and resisting Him.

We rolled off the road with no warning, and all eight of us were thrown about. I was among four in the back of the truck. Another gal and I were both in critical condition and were helicoptered to the hospital within minutes, probably saving our lives. She had a severe brain injury, and her recovery lasted many years. I went into shock, having a C4 spinal cord injury with severe blood loss from road rash to my backside. To date, I haven't fully recovered physically from nerve damage, it remains a part of my life. But the accident spiraled me in a new direction I only dabbled in before. I spent most of the next ten years out of control.

Even after that, I chose to do everything my parents didn't want me to do and had little regard for their input. I was genuinely unhinged and found it relatively easy to find other misguided teenagers since they all hung out in front of the school smoking. The rest of high school flew by, and I was off to college. I quickly found a fraternity that was misguided, and by the next school year, I was kicked out and in trouble with the law.

So, being a smart guy in my mind, I figured I might as well get married and enjoy the good life, right? My new wife and I began our life together with no job, no money, no plan, and no thought of God in our minds. I even snuck off and eloped without thinking of my family. Needless to say, we were young and unable to care for ourselves, and yet we brought a child into the world that was born mentally handicapped.

Well, you can probably guess how that marriage ended, with my well-meaning and energetic mother happy to help end that chapter in my life. My grandfather died of cancer around the same time we divorced, which added additional pain to my life. I didn't see it then, but having custody of my Down Syndrome daughter, Destiny, was from

God. She kept me somewhat grounded even while I spent another 10 years unhinged and still running from God.

I continued doing what was right in my own eyes and was truly blown about by the wind. I believed in God when it was convenient, and I think I liked the idea of having a Heavenly Father, but I knew little of Jesus and His message to mankind: that Jesus is the way, the truth, and the life.

I returned to college several times but was unable to finish. I did, however, complete a shorter technical school and started a career path in civil engineering and land development. That path began with work in Phoenix and then brought me to Bakersfield, then back to Phoenix, and then back to Bakersfield via Santa Monica, Irvine, and Lebec. Don't ever tell God where you think you should live or work, for the Lord, determines our steps.

Looking back over my life, there were two key women who spoke truth and love into my life and nudged me closer to surrendering my life to Christ: my grandmother and my sweet new wife, Maria. They both did this with great gentleness and the love of Christ.

Finally, late in 1999, broken, alone, and confused about life, I sat in the back row at Riverlakes Community Church. I was at the end of my rope when God softened and opened my hard heart. I was finally able and ready to hear His word. I had done this from time to time, but that morning, I heard with my heart. There are no coincidences in God's kingdom, and it just so happened that the message was about unbelief, half-hearted belief, whole-hearted belief in Christ, and the results of rejecting Christ. I finally understood and accepted Christ into my life right then. God's love rushed in and filled me like nothing I ever felt. I now understood that Jesus died on the cross for my sins because he loved me so much and reconciled me to God.

I wasted no time telling everyone I knew about this new life and how God changed me. God did an amazing turnaround in my life. I went from being a selfish know-it-all to one who finally realized that God is the only one who knows it all. I immediately plugged into the wonderful men's ministry at our church and classes as they were offered.

During these changing times in my life, I found the love of my life, Maria. I spent months and many flower arrangements convincing Maria that I genuinely was changed, and she finally agreed to be my wife. We were married a few months later, in March of 2000, bought a home, got a new job, and, by April of 2001, had our baby boy. This was good for me since when we married, I was outnumbered 4 to 1. We had three teenage girls; our niece was 14, my daughter Destiny 15, and my wife's daughter Christina was 16. We do have another son, Manny, who is a couple of years older and was living in Arizona when we were finally married.

Maria and I immediately began teaching 2-year-olds in Sunday school and served in the same class for 2 years. She was then recruited into the children's ministry team and continues to develop, serve, and grow in that ministry. Since I didn't go through the traditional Sunday school classes as a child. God was gracious and allowed me to serve as a leader in our son's Sunday school classes every year as he grew and matured and even graduated through high school ministry.

Over those years, I attended many youth ministry camps as a counselor, and I was also fortunate to witness how God shaped and matured those students and me into leaders and disciples of our Lord Jesus Christ.

Life has certainly not been perfect after coming to Christ, but now I have the assurance of His provision & guidance, whereas before knowing the Lord, I relied on myself and my own strength. I remember this one time so clearly as a young Christian being laid off from my job. I was so excited to see how God was going to show up and provide a new job. I knew He had a plan for my life, and I was fully open to His leading, whatever it would be. I spent many weeks interviewing for jobs and received many offers, but I really wasn't sure what God wanted since he had opened many doors. I finally agreed to a job, and our family went away for Christmas vacation. But while on vacation, I received a better job offer for a sizeable pay increase, so I prayed and asked a mentor for advice. He told me that God does not care how much money I make, but if I do make more, that provides an opportunity to give more to God. So, on the first day of the new job, I went to work and let the company know that I wasn't going to take their job offer after all. This pattern continued for several job changes, and my friends from church would even tease me about switching jobs every year and a half, like clockwork. God kept providing an opportunity for me to give more and more. Now, this pattern of getting more money eventually ended, and the 2008 financial crisis happened. I then ended up having to take a job that was half the pay I had been accustomed to. Perhaps that was God showing His provision for our family.

    I didn't realize it at the time, but my new boss had some addiction issues. God doesn't waste our past failures, and He is gracious. I opened my heart to come alongside Him and see his pain and help in whatever ways I could in that season of our lives. A few years and tears later, my grandmother went to be with the Lord in 2012, and then two years later, my mother passed. I'll never forget one of my grandmother's last words, "It isn't easy getting to heaven." You see, she had been faithfully waiting 25 years after the death of her husband for God to take her home. Our family fondly refers to her as Mother Teresa.

    God has been faithful in providing our needs and fills us with His grace as we serve our family. At the beginning of COVID, our granddaughter, Enez, came to stay with us, who we used to call "little Miss No", so you can guess how those two years went. After Enez graduated high school, she moved back to Arizona to be with her family. This move opened a room for our second oldest grandson, Christian, to move in with us. We consider our home as a gift from the

Lord, and we honor Him as we open our home to our family as needs arise.

Maria and I continue to mature in the Lord; unfortunately, our brokenness has not fully departed during this process, so our continued need for a Savior is a vital part of our lives. Our Lord continues to encourage and strengthen us for the battles we face daily. We seek the Lord with our whole hearts as we submit to His will.

The past few years have been full of trips to Arizona. In July of 2021, my mother-in-law had a heart attack, and my father suffered a stroke. We drove back and forth every few weeks for months, not wanting to miss a chance to be with them both and thinking their time was short on this earth. We had to adjust to monthly trips and then to bi-monthly as best we could manage.

My mother-in-law Angela suffered seven heart attacks before the Lord finally called her home in February 2023. We are only given one life on this earth, and she fought the good fight. Angela and I didn't have the same native tongue, but we both loved the Lord, and our love for each other was bonded. She had a wonderful memorial service full of family who loved her.

Our granddaughter, Enez, fell into another lousy situation this past year in Arizona and has now moved back in with us, adding to our clan. We have had to make new adjustments to our sleeping arrangements, and for now, we do not need to sleep in shifts yet! We will continue to have trials to battle, but we know God is with us, for us, holding us up and guiding us in all things. He is our comfort, our strength, and I choose to lean on Him alone.

I am submitted to God's will, professing my faith in Jesus Christ, our Savior and God, and am very happy to be His child.

Living My Faith Seven Days A Week

Greg Carey
Husband, Father, Printing Press Operator,
IT Support Person

I grew up in West Seattle and attended church from a young age. Mom made sure that all five (three boys and two girls) of the Carey children attended church. She would participate at times, but my dad never did. Even though I attended church, this does not mean that I was an angel by any means. In fact, I was a terror in grade school, constantly getting into fights with other boys from my class. I can't explain the why behind my behavior, whether it was something a guy said or did or just how he blinked his eyes. The bottom line is I don't have any reasonable explanation for being such a hellion, but I was. I had a sister who was two years older than me, but being the oldest boy, I should have been a better example to my younger siblings.

One Sunday, I was sitting in the church youth service, and a man up at the front was speaking. I wish I could remember his name. But one thing I do remember is that he was teaching from John chapter 3 about God's love, how a person could enter heaven, and that if one didn't go to heaven, he or she would go to hell.

As a 13-year-old, this got my attention and started a lot of questions in my mind. The man in front spoke for three Sundays in a row of God's love, heaven, and hell. Each week, I stayed after class and asked my teacher questions, who patiently answered all my concerns. On the third Sunday, I prayed the sinner's prayer and asked Jesus to be the Lord of my life. It's a very simple prayer. It goes like this:

"Dear God, I know that I am a sinner. I know that I need a Savior, one who can save me from the sin in my life. I know that Jesus came to be that Savior, that he died on the cross for me. I ask that he come into my life and help me turn away from sin, to cleanse me so that I can have a place in heaven."

After praying these words, there didn't seem to be any significant change in my life. There were no fireworks, visions, or grand happenings coming my way because of my newfound faith. But one thing did happen, which I am sure God had a hand in. I stopped fighting at school.

One verse has stuck with me ever since. It is John 3, verse 16: "For God so loved the world that he gave his only begotten Son, that whosoever believeth in him should not perish but have everlasting life." This verse assured me then, and still does today, that I am saved from an eternity in hell and that I have a place in heaven because of Jesus' sacrificing act of love for me and for all people the world over.

That angry part of me, that fighting part, seemed to fade away after that. I can't remember if it was a sudden change or something that happened gradually, but I didn't fight with other boys as I had before. I continued attending church each Sunday, and soon, I was also going to the mid-week youth meetings. Gradually, I started helping with other church activities, such as church programs for the younger children during the week. I also taught a class for younger children on Sundays. However, when away from church, I didn't talk about Jesus or being saved at all. My friends at school were, therefore, unaware that I attended church on Sundays. My life, as seen by others, wasn't radically changed. I was a Sunday Christian by all accounts, doing Christian things when at church but living like everyone else when not at church—but not fighting for that part of my life was over!

It was in 1971, my junior year in high school, when a new youth pastor came that I started to see that God wanted more from me, more of my life than one day a week. My understanding of the Bible increased, especially my knowledge of Jesus, his life, death, and resurrection. I could see, for the first time, that God saw me as an everyday Christian in his kingdom, not just one day a week. Along with this, God also wanted me to pay attention to his Word, the Bible, all seven days of the week, which I began to do from that point on.

One result of my newfound love of Jesus caused concern within my own family. But I didn't know about it until many years later. That result was that my father, who was a strong but quiet man, became somewhat concerned about the amount of time I was spending at church. He did some investigating of this newfound religion that I had embraced. Around the same time as I was finding my new life in Jesus, there were religious groups that seemed to offer proper living and wise teachings but weren't connected to a mainline church. I am sure he was worried that I had fallen into one of these groups, which he felt would sooner or later cause me grief in my life.

I didn't find out about all this until after he had died at the young age of 58. I found out when my parents' high school friend, Elva, came to see me three days after dad's funeral. Elva and her husband Dave didn't attend the church I did, but I believe that Dad knew that Elva and Dave were churchgoers. Dad felt comfortable enough to go to them with questions about his eldest son's involvement with this church youth group. I don't know how much of my walk with Jesus or how much Dave and Elva's words about Jesus had an impact on my dad, but Elva did tell me later that before he died, dad had come to believe in Jesus and had prayed that simple sinner's prayer which I had prayed at the age of 13. A prayer you might consider if you haven't already prayed such a prayer. And although I never felt my life dramatically changed that much after receiving Christ, it did from God's perspective, for He made me into a new person.

Living through Legalism and Licentiousness

Kent McClain
Minister, Teacher, Superintendent, Writer/Author

During Easter vacation while in college, I was a part of the singing group that provided the music for Campus Crusade for Christ during one of their crusades at Balboa Island in California. Our group was called the Something Singers, not because we thought we were something, but because we had something to sing about, Jesus Christ.

Every night during this Easter week, there was a program presented by Crusade (short for Campus Crusade for Christ) at the Balboa Pavilion, which seated about 1000 kids. Our group would lead things off with some songs, and then Andre Cole, a well-known magician, would come up and perform several awe-inspiring illusions, which led to a final one that set the stage for him sharing the Gospel at the end. After that, a Crusade leader named Linus came up and introduced a student who shared how they came to know Christ. The testimonies shared by these students got more and more interesting and dramatic as the week went along. Many came to know Christ because of them.

As the week came to an end, Linus asked if I would be one of those students sharing a testimony. I don't know why he asked me; I just barely knew him. Perhaps it was because, aside from singing at night in the Pavilion with my singing group, I joined Crusade during the day to share the gospel with students hanging out on the beach. Anyway, I agreed.

One of my friends, Ralph, who was with me this week, said, "What are you going to share, Kent? Your testimony is dull at best." After thinking about it for a few hours, I came up with what I would say. Just before walking up that night to give my testimony, Ralph grabbed me by the arm and again said, "What in the world are you going to share?" "You'll see!" I said.

Andre Cole finished his last illusion, sharing the Gospel at the end as he usually did, and then I was introduced by Linus. I began by saying, "I don't know if many of you know this, but a few years ago, I was in the Hell's Angels. One night, while riding my Harley down Newport Boulevard during an intense rainstorm, I lost control of my bike. I slid all the way through the intersection and right into the front door of a small little church. As I skidded down the aisle, the preacher was giving an altar call. I raised my hand and stated, "I believe!"

The high school and college crowd was not laughing as I thought they would but appeared a little spellbound and in awe. Then I continued, "That sounds like a very dramatic testimony, does it not? But to be honest with you, I really came to know Christ when I was five years old at the altar of my dad's church. Hopefully, you can see that you don't have to have a dramatic testimony to come into the kingdom of God. All you need to do is to put your faith in Christ whether on a motorcycle, at the altar of a church, on Newport Beach, or in the quiet of your own heart somewhere else." Linus then came to the podium and gave a great concluding message, and many came to know Christ that night.

Frankly, how I came to know Christ as Lord and Savior was not very dramatic, but what was dramatic was how Jesus took care of me in the turbulent days ahead while growing up. I was only five years old when I asked Jesus into my heart. But before I tell you about this conversion experience of mine, let me share a little about my family. My dad was a Nazarene Pastor in Pasadena, California, and his wife, Ernestine, was not just a faithful pastor's wife but a strong and visible influence in the church. I had an older brother, but he, like me, was too young to make much of a difference in the church. However, my dad did have my brother sing in several of his services, for he had a very good voice and used me as a ring bearer at the weddings he performed.

The morning I asked Jesus into my heart, as I look back, was a real confession of faith. It was on a Sunday at the end of one of my dad's sermons. As he concluded his last words, my dad asked if anyone wanted to come down to the altar and receive Christ. A few did, and while they did, I felt an emotional tug from the Lord to do the same. So, I got up out of my seat and walked down to the altar where my dad stood. When I got there, surprisingly, he asked me, "Kent, do you know what you are doing?" I said, "Yes, dad, I do." He hesitated a bit but then responded, "Well, then, Kent, pray as I pray, 'Jesus forgive me of my sins, and come into my life and be my Lord.' And I did.

As I look back on that morning, it was truly the moment I walked into the kingdom of God. Although I was so young, I meant what I said at the altar and then followed up later by praying the Lord's prayer every night before going to sleep—that is, until I got older and replaced it with other prayers.

The dramatic part of my conversion story began two years later when my dad was pastoring another Nazarene Church in Louisville, Kentucky. I was still very young at the time but old enough to hear what was going on between my dad and mother. My room at home was right next to theirs, and the arguing and screaming that went on could not be escaped. Soon, my mom was packing up my brother and me to return to California, where my brother and I were born and first grew up. What was the issue with this family breakup? My dad had an affair with the church secretary, and my mother could not forgive him for doing so. The marriage was over as far as she was concerned, and so was our family as we had known it.

Over the next few years, verbal battles continued between my mom and dad, for he also returned to California after serving a few years in the Navy as a chaplain. He tried to see my brother and me from time to time, but to no avail because of my mother's bitterness. In all of this, I never gave up my relationship with the Lord because the Nazarene church I attended after returning to California was a constant help to both my brother and me. And, of course, the Lord never left either of our sides.

My dad eventually returned to the pastoral ministry, but this time around, he switched denominations, one that would accept his divorce. On the other hand, my mother did not attend church again for many years but did encourage my brother and me to keep going, which we did. Without the Lord in my life, starting at that altar and the ministry of those wonderful church members and Sunday school teachers, I hate to say how I might have turned out.

It was only while attending college that I was finally able to spend some time with my dad because my mother had lost control of that part of my life. During those times together, I really got to know him, and all that really went on in Kentucky. All I can say is that he was not totally at fault, and my mother caused a lot of what happened. He did have an affair, which was wrong, but he was not as bad as my mom made him out to be. And I believed my dad because I had similar conflicts and issues with her while growing up.

As I was getting to know my dad and loving him in the process, he died of a heart attack. He was only 50 years old when he passed away, but the night before he went to be with the Lord, he called me from his hospital bed. During our conversation, he asked for my forgiveness for all that had happened, and of course, I readily gave it to him. Then I told him before hanging up, "Dad, I love you, always have, and always will." I sensed tears from him on the other end and heard a sigh of relief before hanging up.

According to his brother, who was there with him at the time, he went to be with the Lord two hours after that conversation. His brother, my uncle CA (Charles Allen), whom I was named after, said it had been a long time since he had seen my dad in that much peace. And I guess that's what having Christ can do: bring peace to a life that is very young, like me, or to someone like my dad, lying in a hospital bed, ready to pass on.

I soon graduated from Pasadena Nazarene College. During my years at PC (short for Pasadena Nazarene College), I started two Christian ministries, Campus Crusade being one of them. Since PC was a Christian College, there was no one to really share Christ with on campus, so some other student leaders and I helped train and took a group of fellow students downtown to Pasadena City College to share the Gospel.

However, I did rebel against many of the rules and regulations while at PC from time to time. In doing so, I mostly made fun of the legalism I saw on my campus and even wrote a book about it a few years ago called *What Was I Thinking?*

One thing I did, for instance, was skip the daily chapels as much as possible. I did this in different ways over the four years without getting caught, for if I had been, it could have led to being suspended. During my first year of chapel, the oversight committee allowed you to choose what row you wanted to sit in, but you had to stay in that seat the rest of the year. So, a few of us with similar views about legalism sat next to each other.

At the beginning of chapel, sign-in sheets were passed out to each row, and if you didn't log in, that would count as an absence. So, chapel began, which ended up being more and more boring and repetitive. Occasionally, there was an interesting speaker. The four guys I was sitting next to had had it with chapel after about 4 weeks. I, therefore, devised a scheme where each of us could skip at least one day each week by simply signing in for the one taking a break. It worked, and no one was the wiser. Then we moved into skipping two days a week as time went along, then 3 days, and then 4. We got to the point where each of us had to go to chapel just once a week, signing in for the others. The oversight committee did not catch on or simply didn't care as long as they had their signatures. Then, after a few months of this, there were 5 others in our row who started doing the same. I think one day, on a Friday, which was my day to show up and sign in for the others, there were only two of us sitting in the row, but 10 signatures on the sign-in sheet. They changed the system the following year.

After PC, I went to the University of Wyoming to work on my master's degree. Over the next two years, I continued helping Campus Crusade for Christ by starting a new work there. But instead of battling legalism, I battled with the opposite: no rules at all. This led to me dealing with licentiousness to a level I was not prepared for, but I kept my faith throughout my time there.

After Wyoming, I returned to Los Angeles to intern at the Jesus Christ Light and Power House, a ministry located on the UCLA campus. Hal Lindsey (author of the Late Great Planet Earth), Bill Counts, and an old friend from Easter Week at Balboa Island, Linus Morris, were my mentors and taught me a great deal about God's grace during those two years. It was there that I met my future wife, Myrna, whom I have been with ever since.

After marrying, Myrna helped me in my first youth ministry in Seattle at Hillcrest Presbyterian Church. While in Seattle, we started our own Jesus Christ Light and Power House on the University of Washington campus. These first days of marriage and ministry together were great in so many ways. We saw many young people come to know the Lord and then go off and do ministries of their own in various ways.

After Seattle, Myrna and I served the Lord in various ministries and school positions for the next 40 or so years. Some of those positions and responsibilities included other youth ministries, a Children and Family Life ministry, a Men's and Assimilation ministry, an associate pastorate, a senior pastorate, a schoolteacher, a principal, and a Christian school Superintendent. Added to my degrees at PC and the University of Wyoming came other graduate degrees and necessary accompanying credentials.

All these experiences, which began when I received Christ as a young boy, were very joyous, rewarding, and heartwarming overall. Yet there were some along the way that were downright hard, defeating, and frustrating. There were those we met and worked with along the way who were very loving and Godly and those who were not. I guess I will just have to wait till heaven to work out things with them.

Both Myrna and I are retired now, living in Boise near our daughter, son-in-law, and their two young children. They are all Christ-followers. My son is a missionary in the country of Georgia, near Ukraine and the Russian border. He, his wife, and their two older children work tirelessly every day to bring people to Christ in that part of the world. Myrna and I help them when we can.

In addition to the small Bible studies and children's Sunday school classes Myrna and I have conducted over these past 10 years, I have also done a lot of writing. In my writing, which now include a few hundred articles and seven different Christian-based books, if there were only one lesson I am allowed to end up sharing, it would be that there are loving Christ-followers everywhere, no matter the church or denomination. And I thank God for them, for I believe they really are, in essence, the kind of people God truly wanted on earth to serve as His church.

Finally, I thank God for forgiving grace, protection, and never-ending presence over the years, for without Him, I would have been lost several times over.

Epilogue

"For God so loved the world, that He gave His only begotten Son, that whoever believes in Him shall not perish, but have eternal life." John 3:16

As you have read through these stories, you saw that each of these nine men made a life-changing decision to respond to Christ's call to salvation. Today, they are all in God's kingdom and following Him as best they can for the remaining days they have left on earth.

If you have never made this decision yourself, I implore you to do so while there is time. All you need do is believe in Jesus as the Son of God, make Him the Lord of your life, and repent of your sins.

One of our writers, Greg Carey, mentioned a Sinner's Prayer in his story. It is repeated below, to help you know what to say to God and yourself if you truly want to be saved and come into God's Kingdom.

The Sinner's Prayer

God in heaven, I come to you in Jesus' name. I acknowledge to You that I am a sinner, and I am sorry for my sins and the life that I have lived; I need your forgiveness.

I believe that your only begotten Son Jesus Christ shed His precious blood on the cross at Calvary and died for my sins, and I am now willing to turn from my sin.

You said in the Bible that if we confess the Lord our God and believe in our hearts that God raised Jesus from the dead, we shall be saved.

Right now, I confess Jesus as my Lord. With my heart, I believe that God raised Jesus from the dead. This very moment, I accept Jesus Christ as my personal Savior, and according to His Word, I am saved. Amen.

If you have prayed this prayer, then let one of these nine writers know, or let me (Kent McClain) know, for I would like to pray with you and talk to you further.

My email is kent@tmoments.com

A word from the publisher:

Destinée Media publishes both fiction and nonfiction and aims to bring a fresh perspective to spirituality and culture.

At Destinée Media we seek to operate by faith in God within a Biblical/Christian worldview. We hope to inspire "culture making" by promoting ideas that will contribute to Christ being understood as Lord of the whole of life, which is to be marked by redemption and renewal.

We are committed to reflecting carefully on vital matters for the church, academy and society, while aiming to keep a personal and intimate dimension of the Christian life in view.

We thank you for your interest in our materials and hope that you find them both relevant and challenging. Please share your thoughts with us: www.destineemedia.com

www.ingramcontent.com/pod-product-compliance
Lightning Source LLC
Chambersburg PA
CBHW060539080526
44586CB00012B/796